AF506463

Happy and Healed: Black Women Adult Coloring Book | Stress Relief, Relaxation and Self Love

Created and Designed by: Latoya Nicole
Illustrated by: Shakira Rivers

ISBN: 979-8-9856190-2-7

For more information, visit us
online at www.entrepreneurscolortoo.com

This book
belongs to:

____

COLOR TEST PAGE

Dear ______________________________,

You are creative, innovative, and capable of achieving greatness. You have faced lots of challenges throughout your life, but you have always persevered and overcome them.

As you travel through life, remember to never forget your worth and value. Believe in yourself, your abilities, and your dreams. Know that your voice matters.

It is important to take care of yourself and prioritize your mental, physical, and emotional health. Surround yourself with those who uplift and support you.

Remember that you are not alone, and it is okay to ask for help when needed.

Seek out resources, support systems, and communities that can help you on your journey.

Most of all, never forget that you are deserving of love, respect, and happiness. You have the power to create the life you want and deserve, and you are capable of achieving anything you set your mind to.

Keep going and inspiring others with your strength, resilience, and beauty.

Before you begin let's take a few moments to just breathe.

1. **Choose a comfortable position.**
2. **Inhale for a count of 5 through your mouth.**
3. **Exhale for a count of 5 out through your nose.**
4. **Continue this breathing pattern for at least a few minutes.**

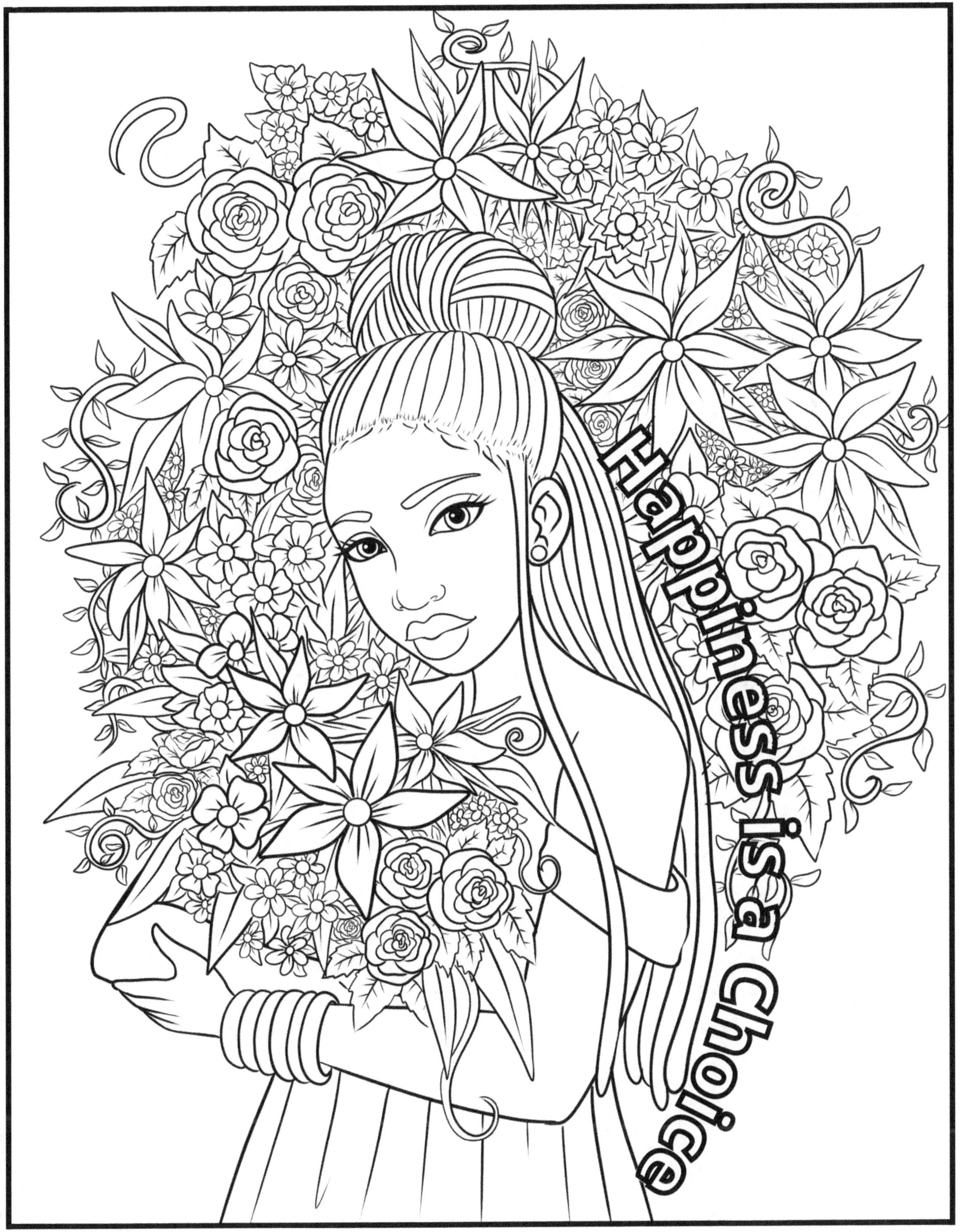
Happiness is a choice

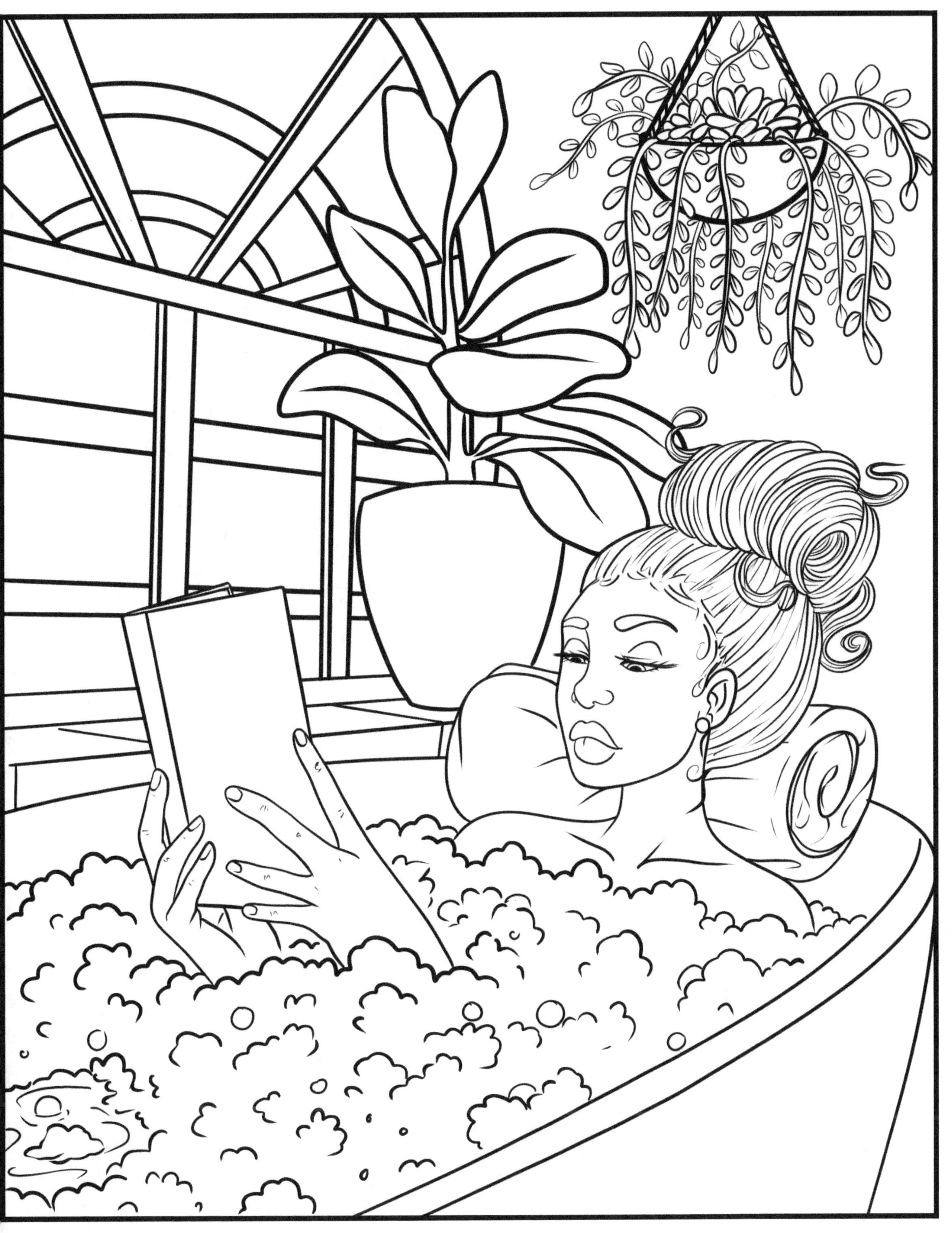

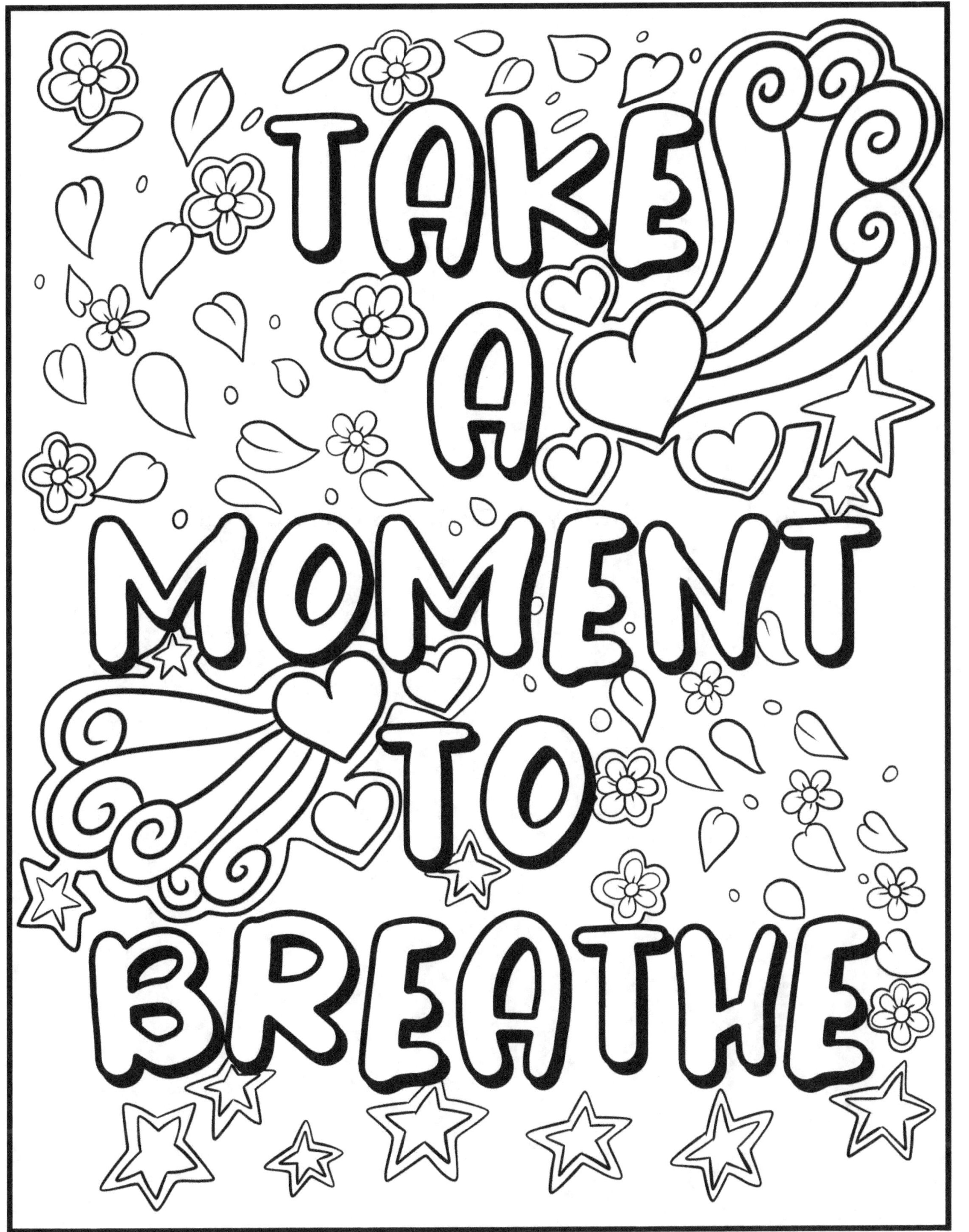

TAKE A MOMENT TO BREATHE

Always laugh when you can. It's cheap medicine.

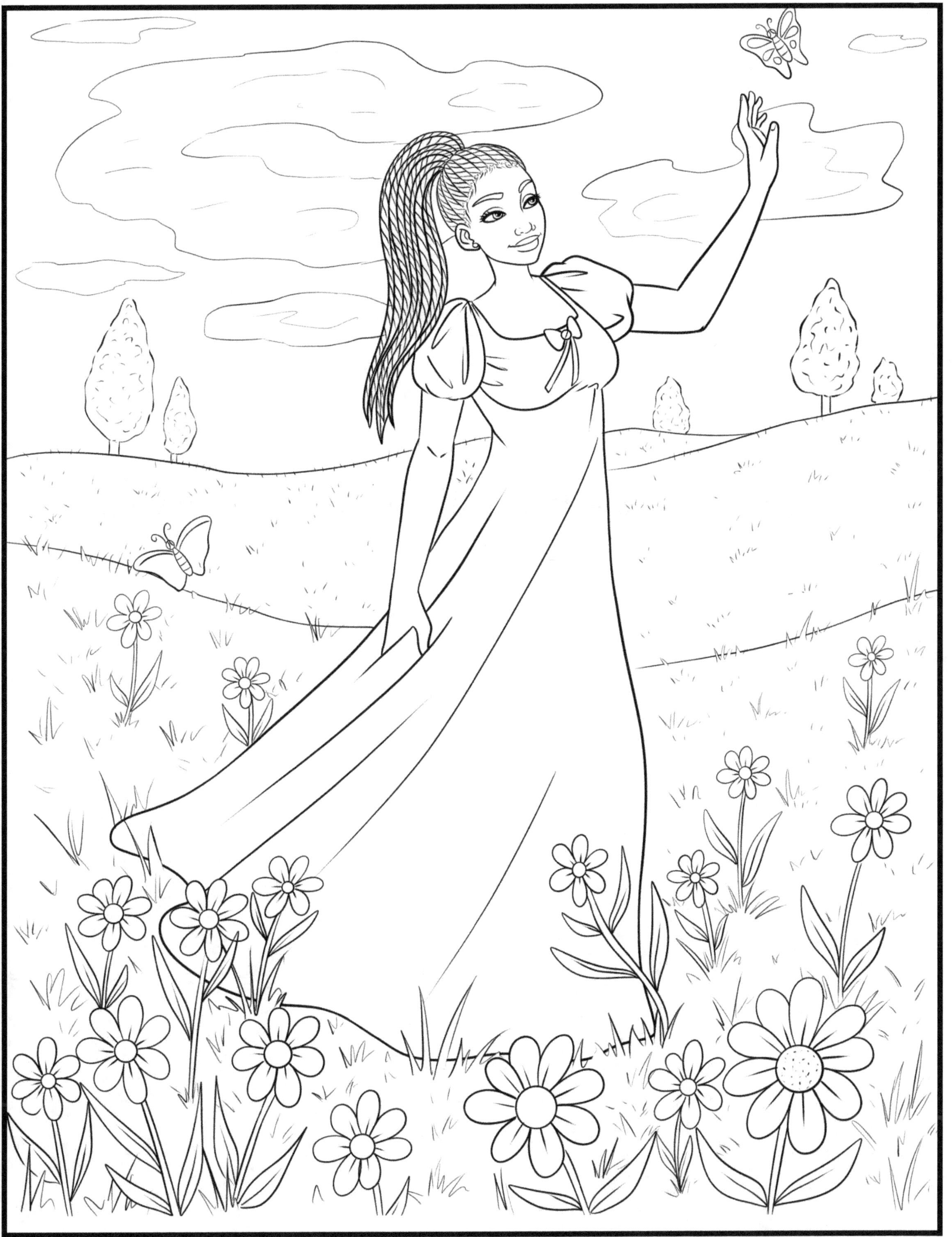

Find relationships that challenge and inspire you.

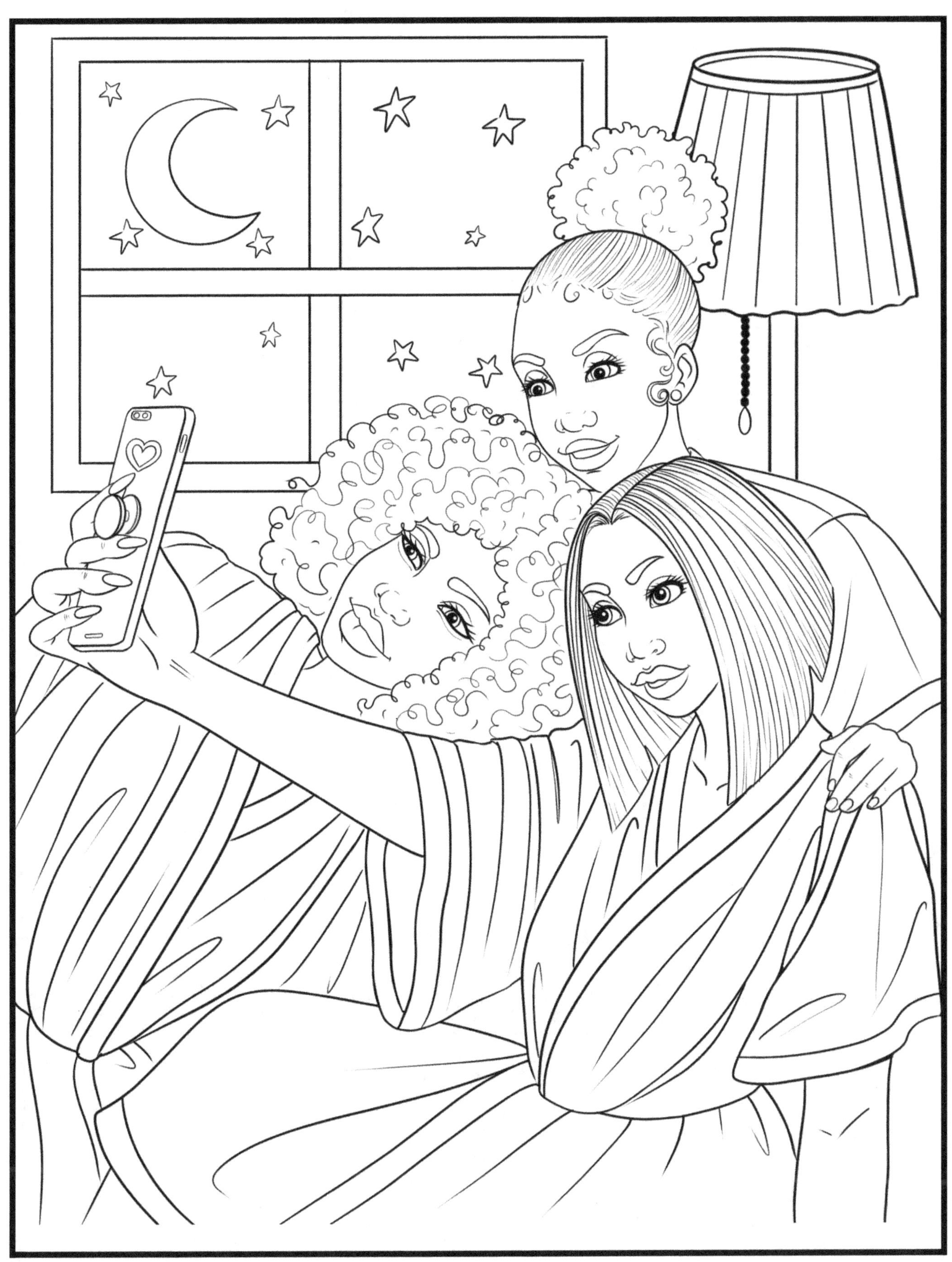

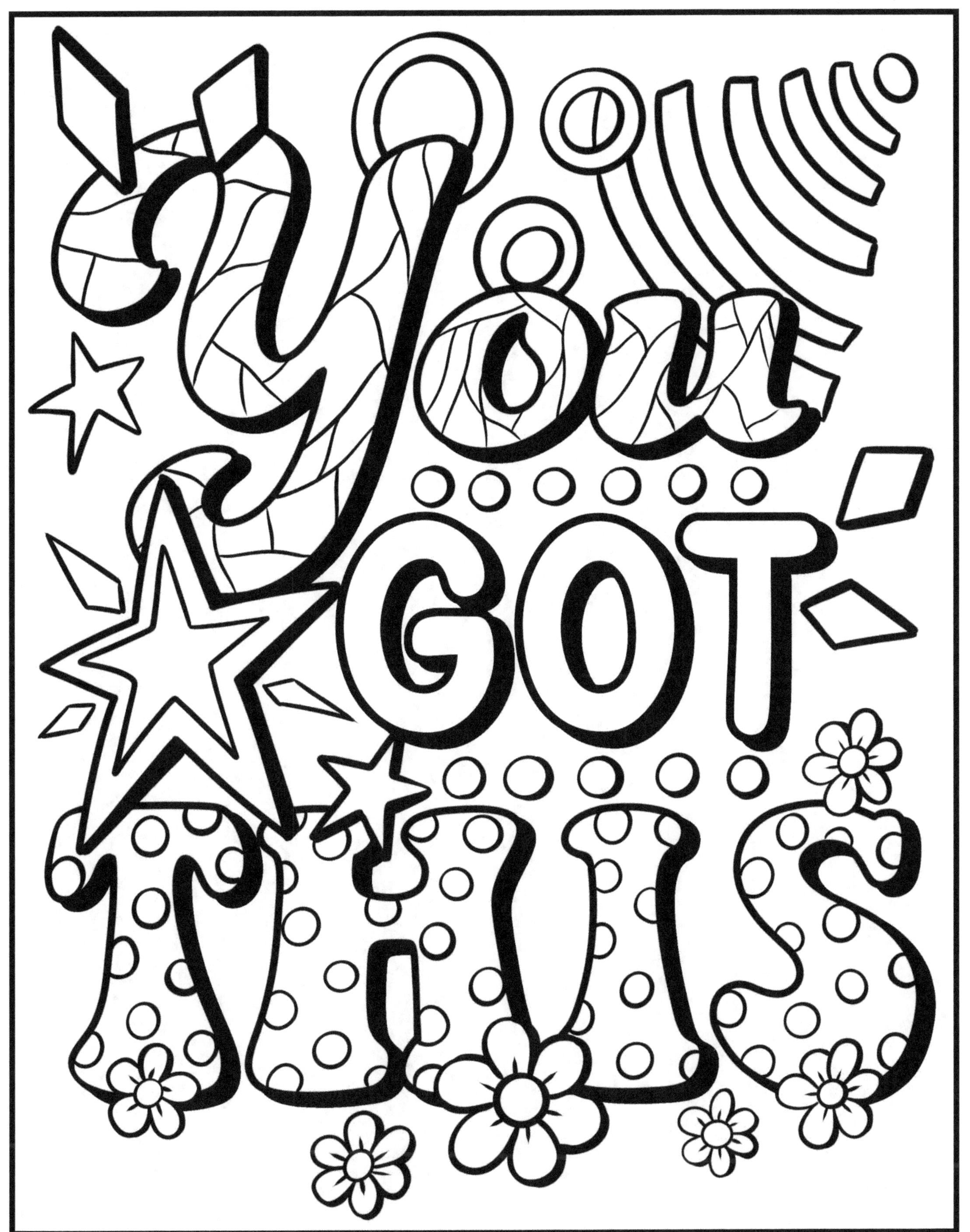
You
GOT
THIS

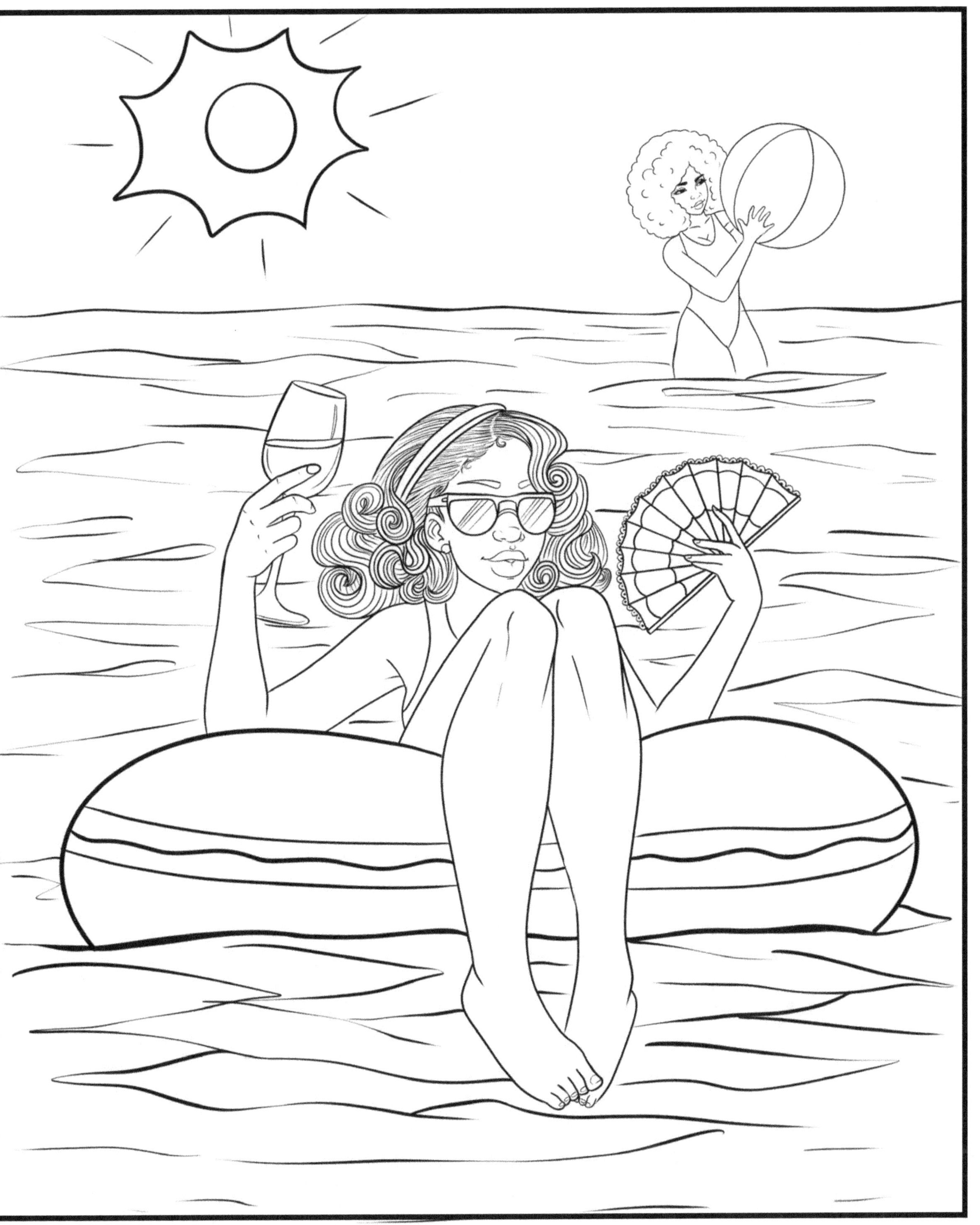

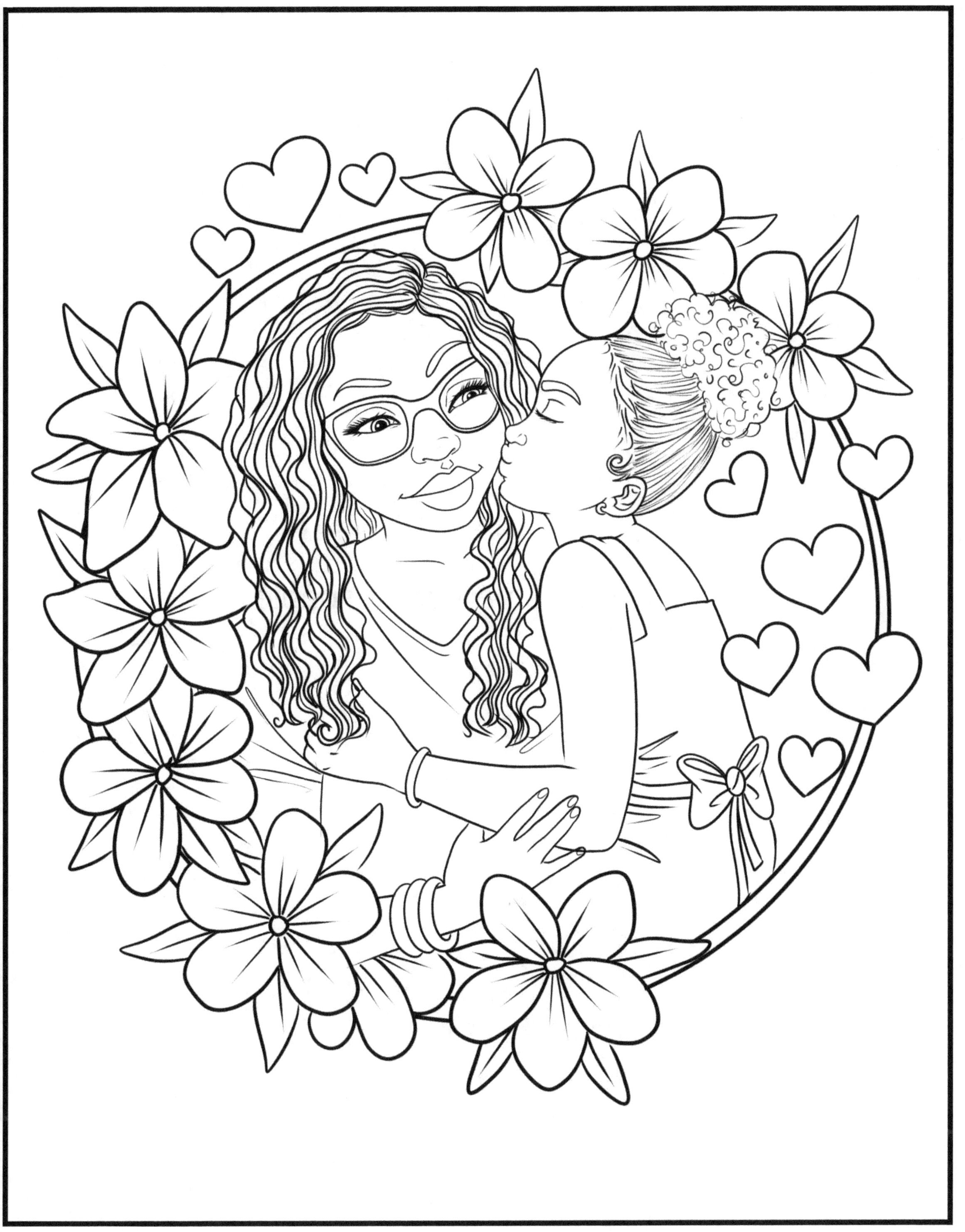

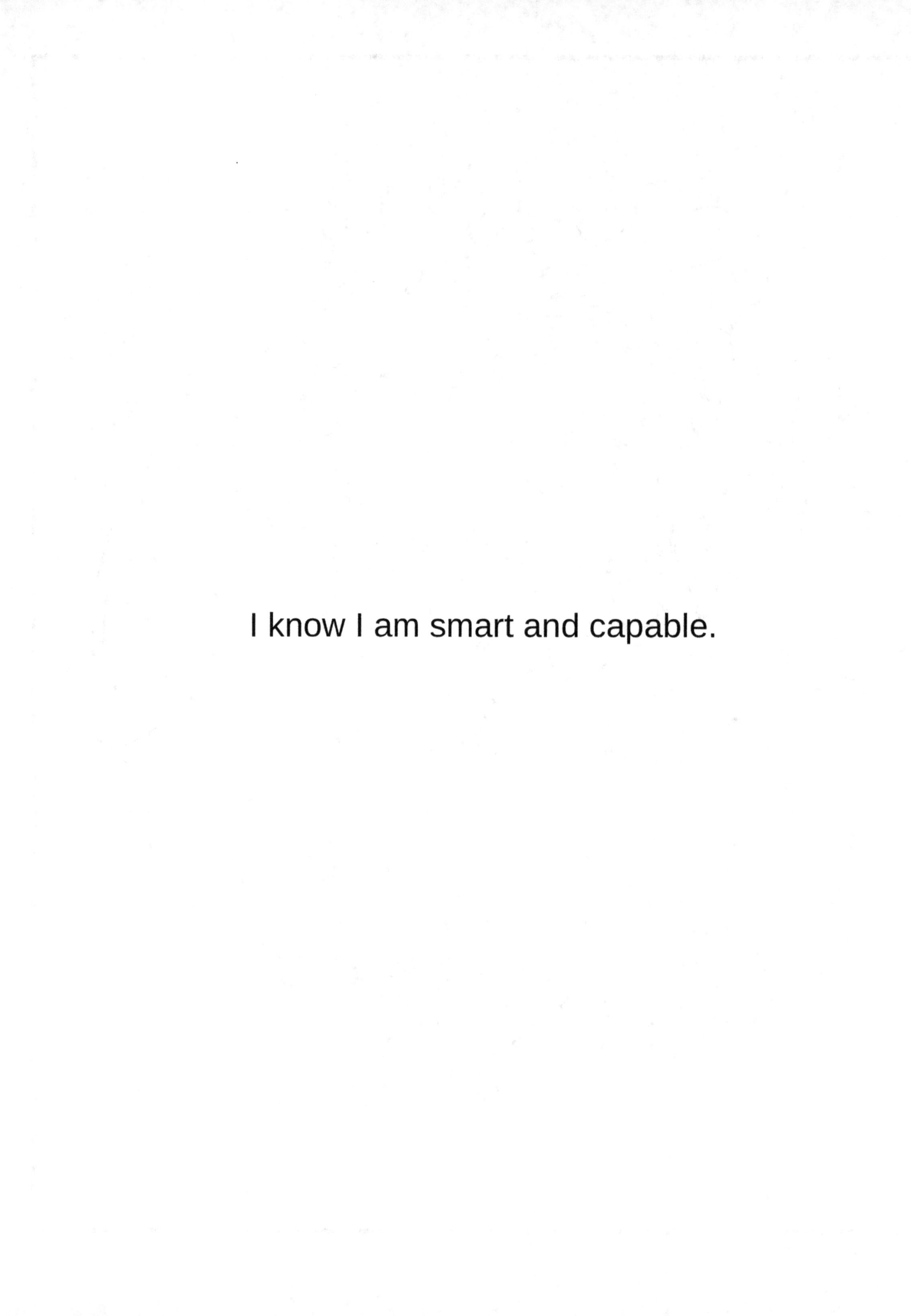

I know I am smart and capable.

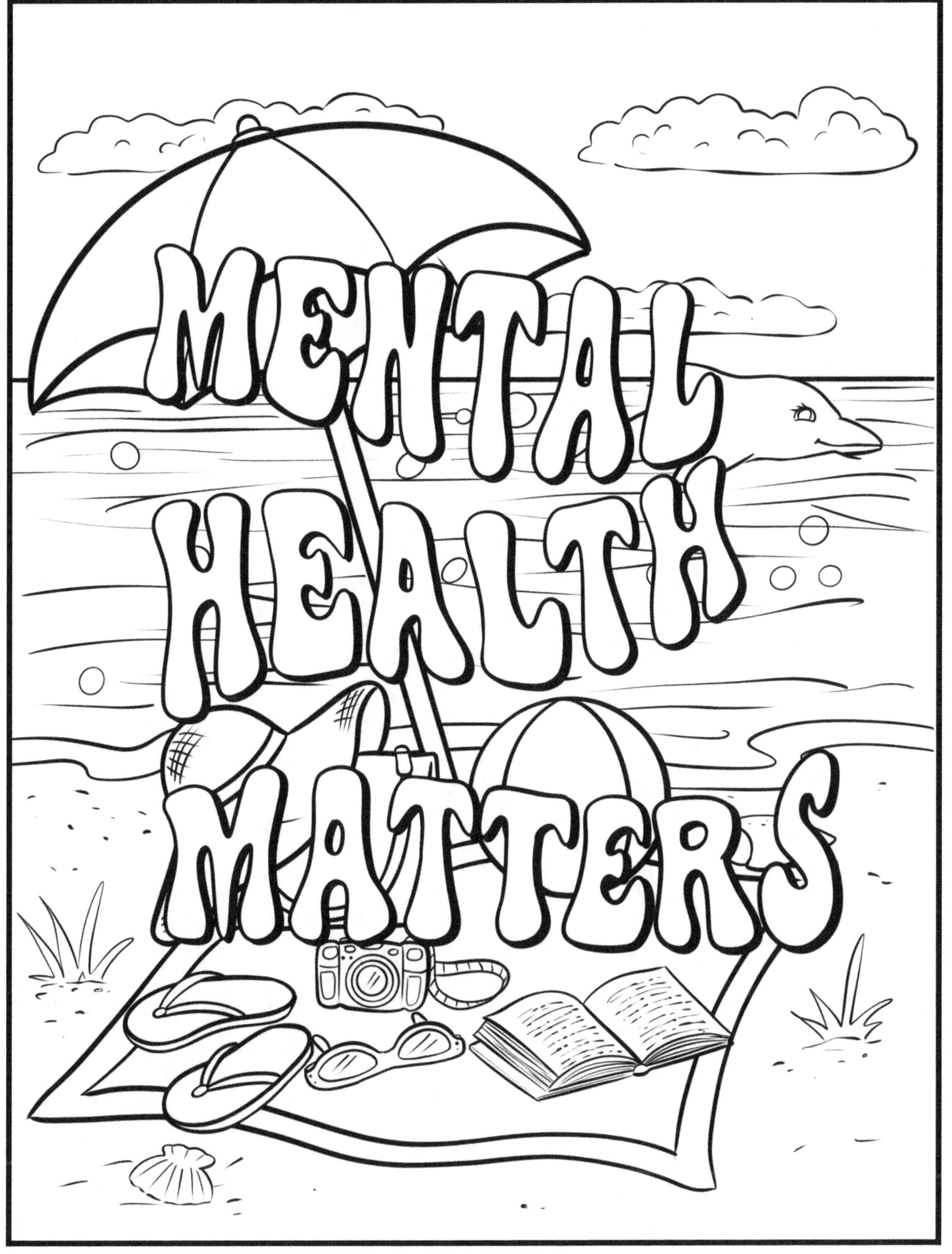

MENTAL
HEALTH
MATTERS

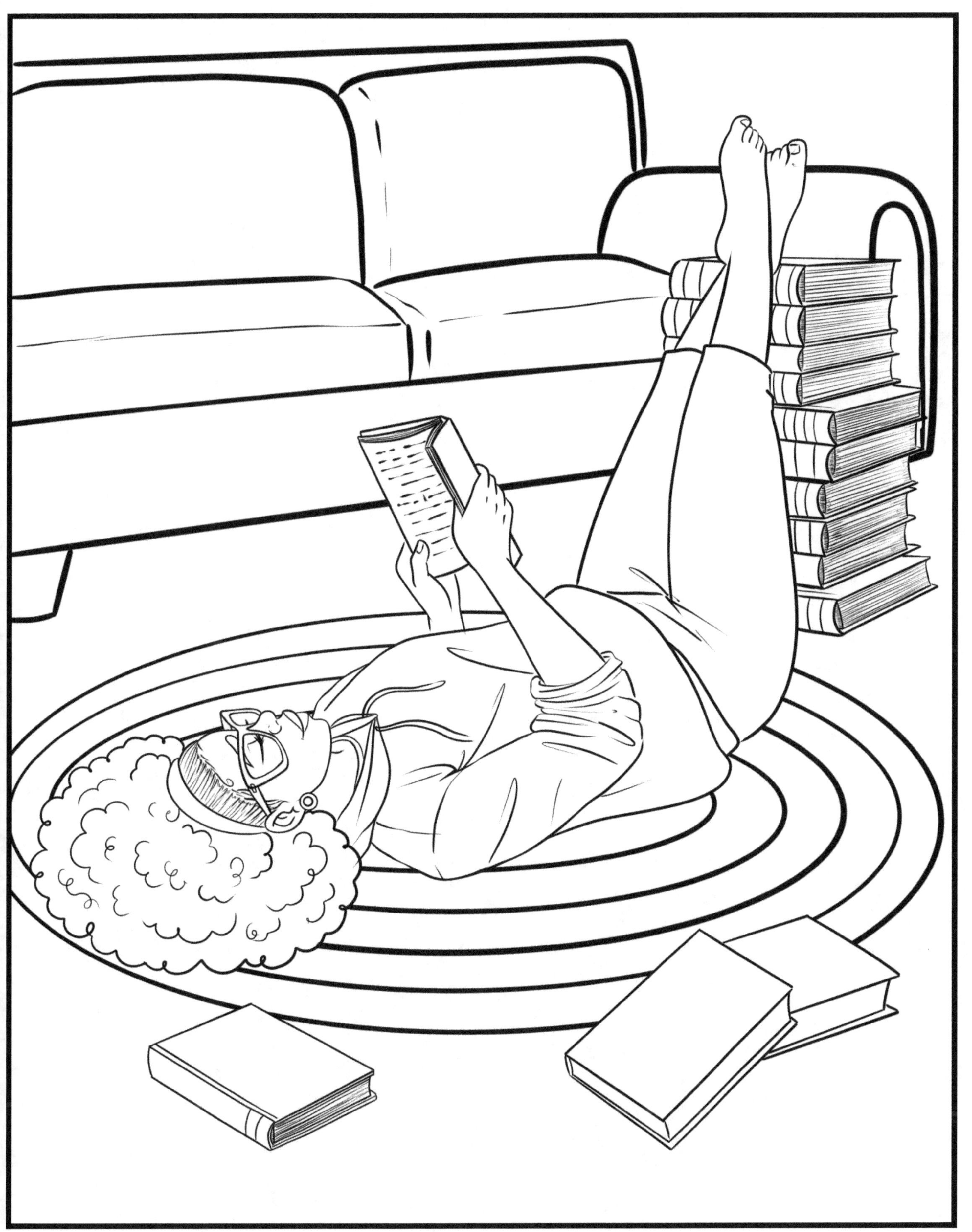

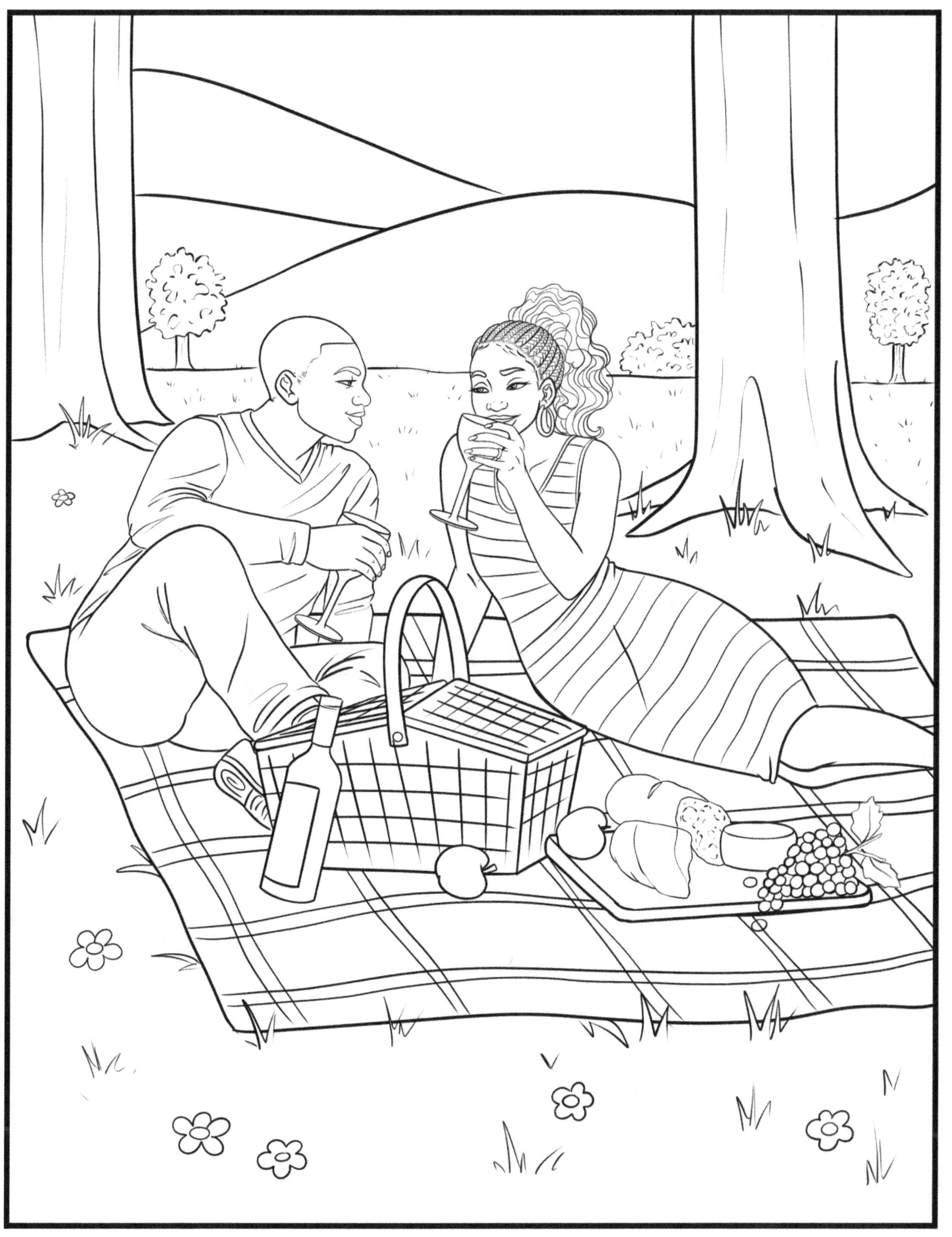

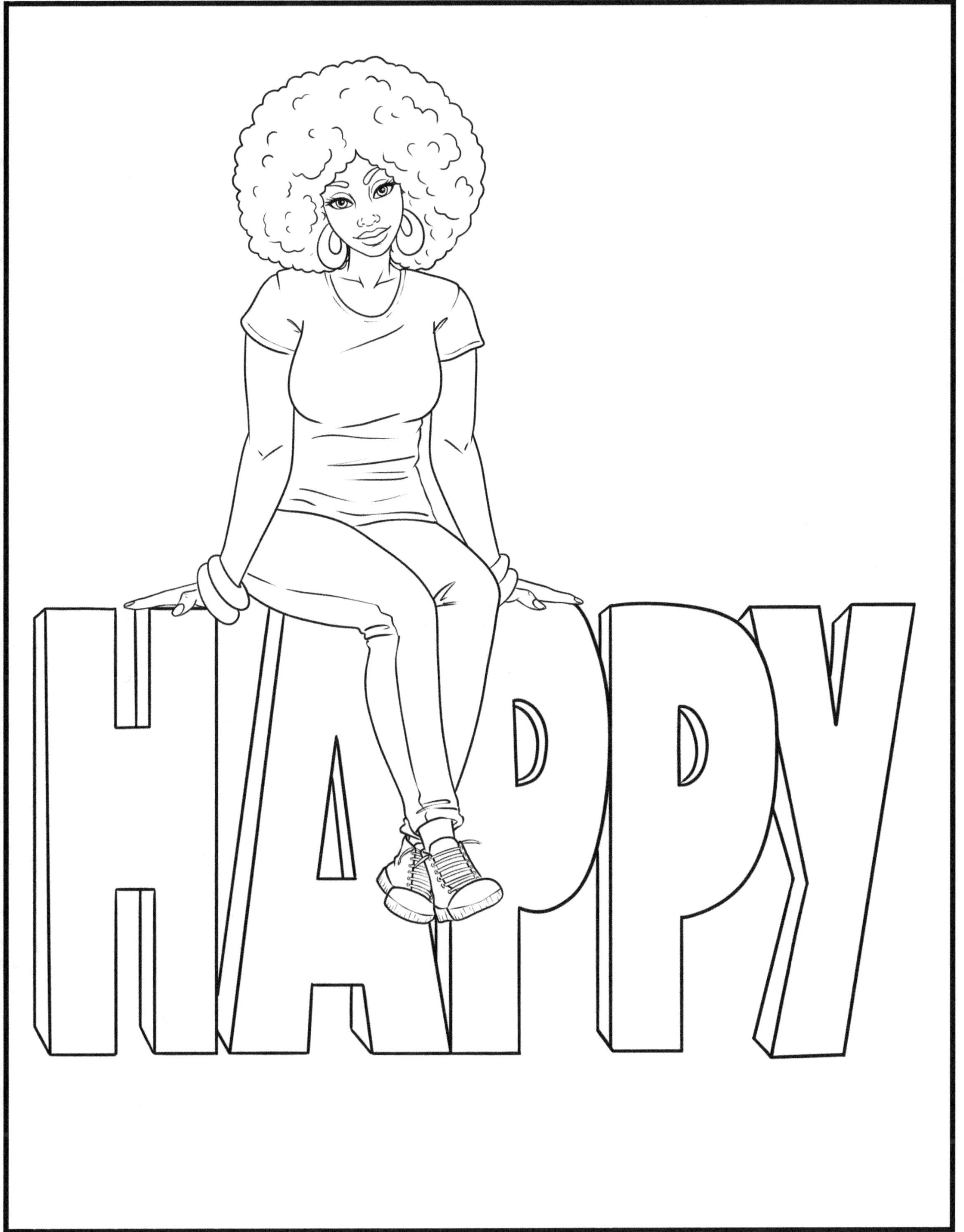
HAPPY

I feel free to be myself.

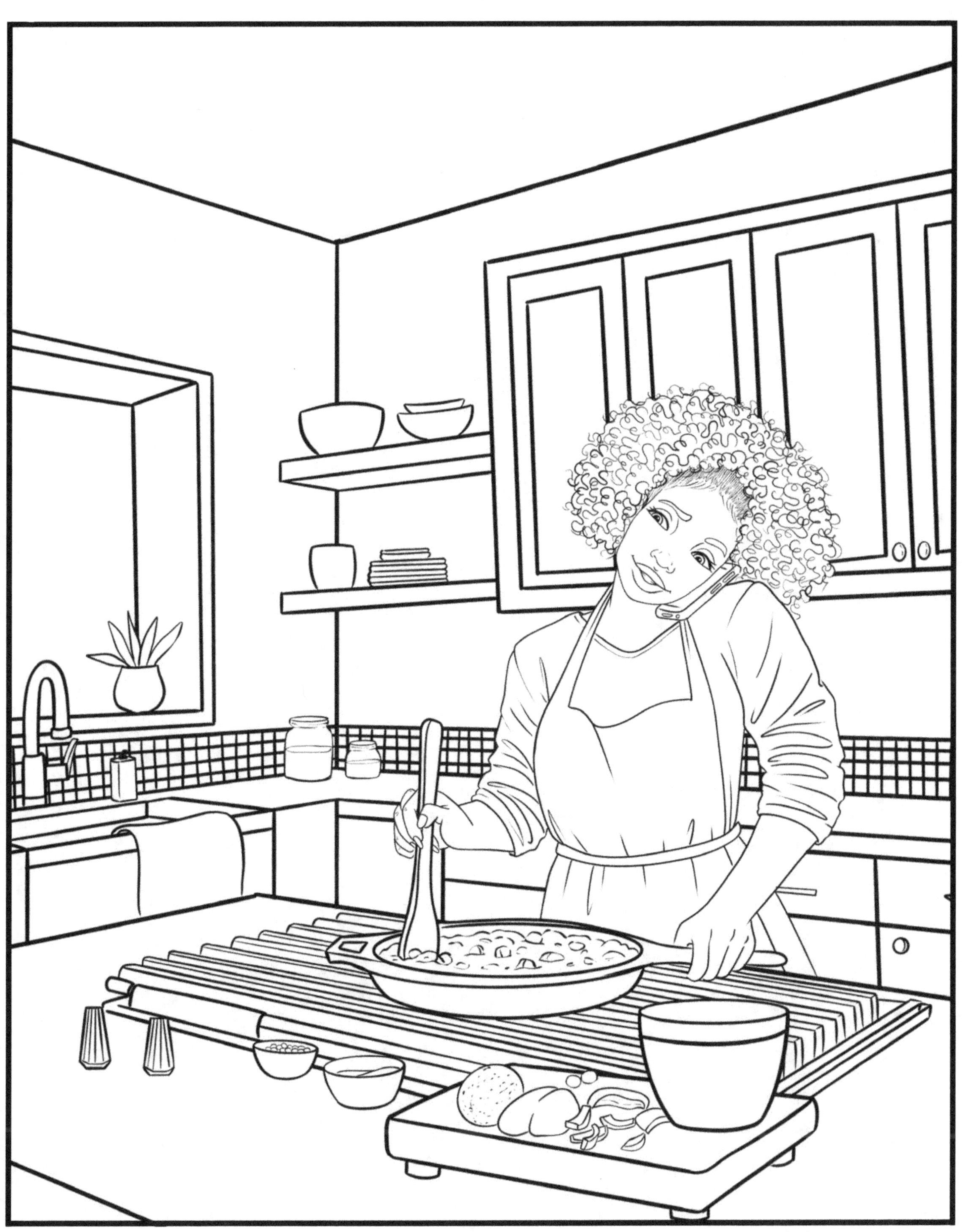

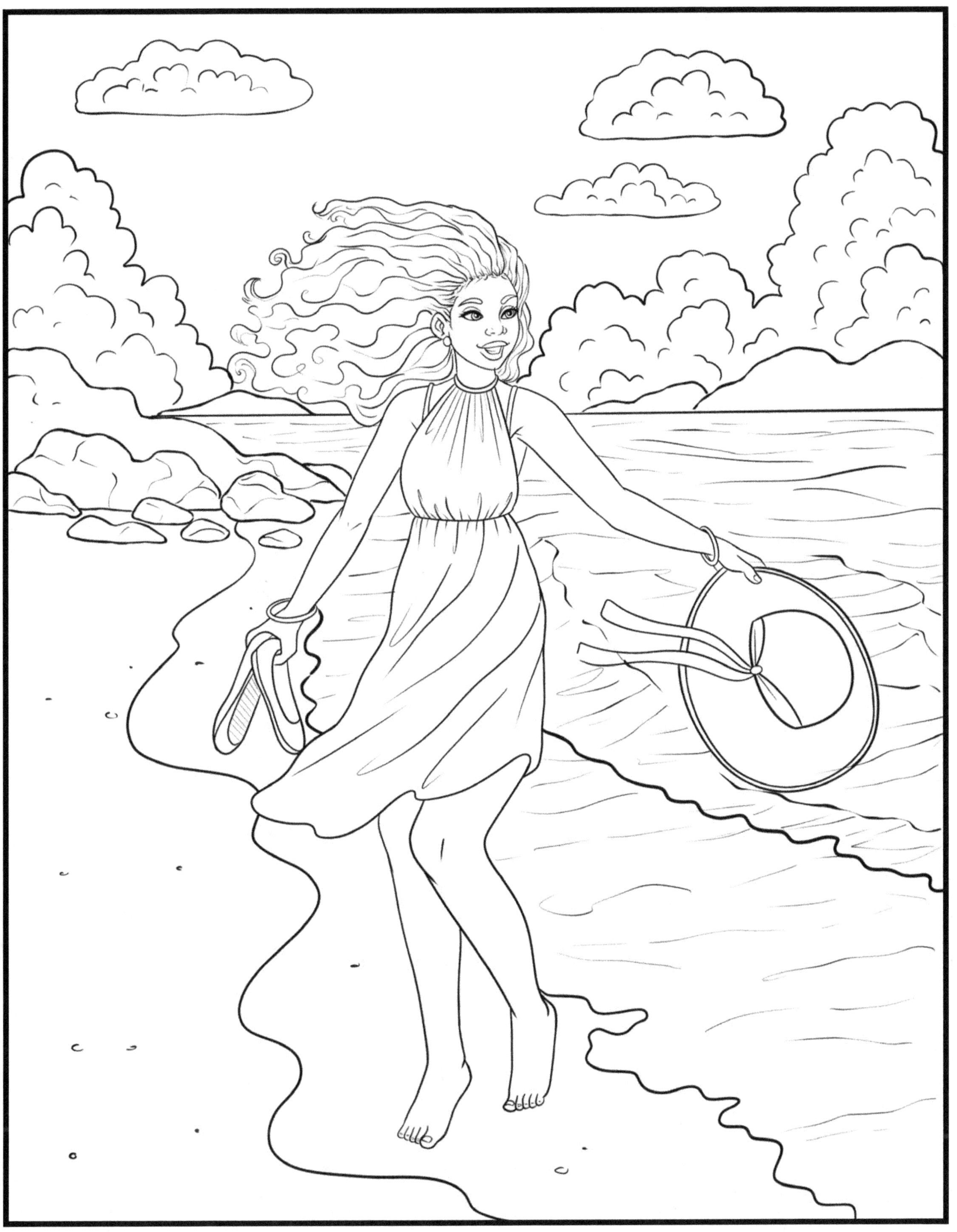

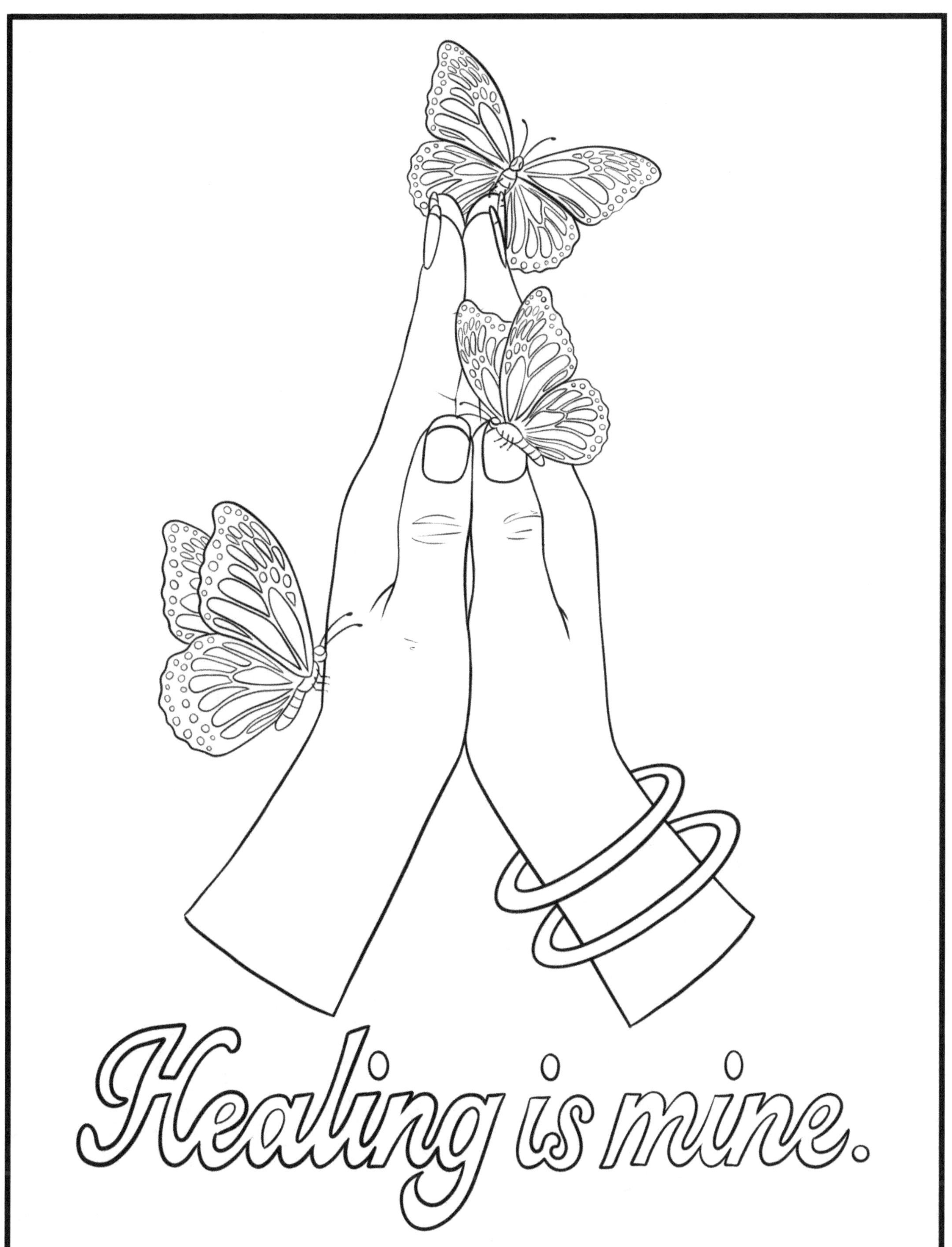

Healing is mine.

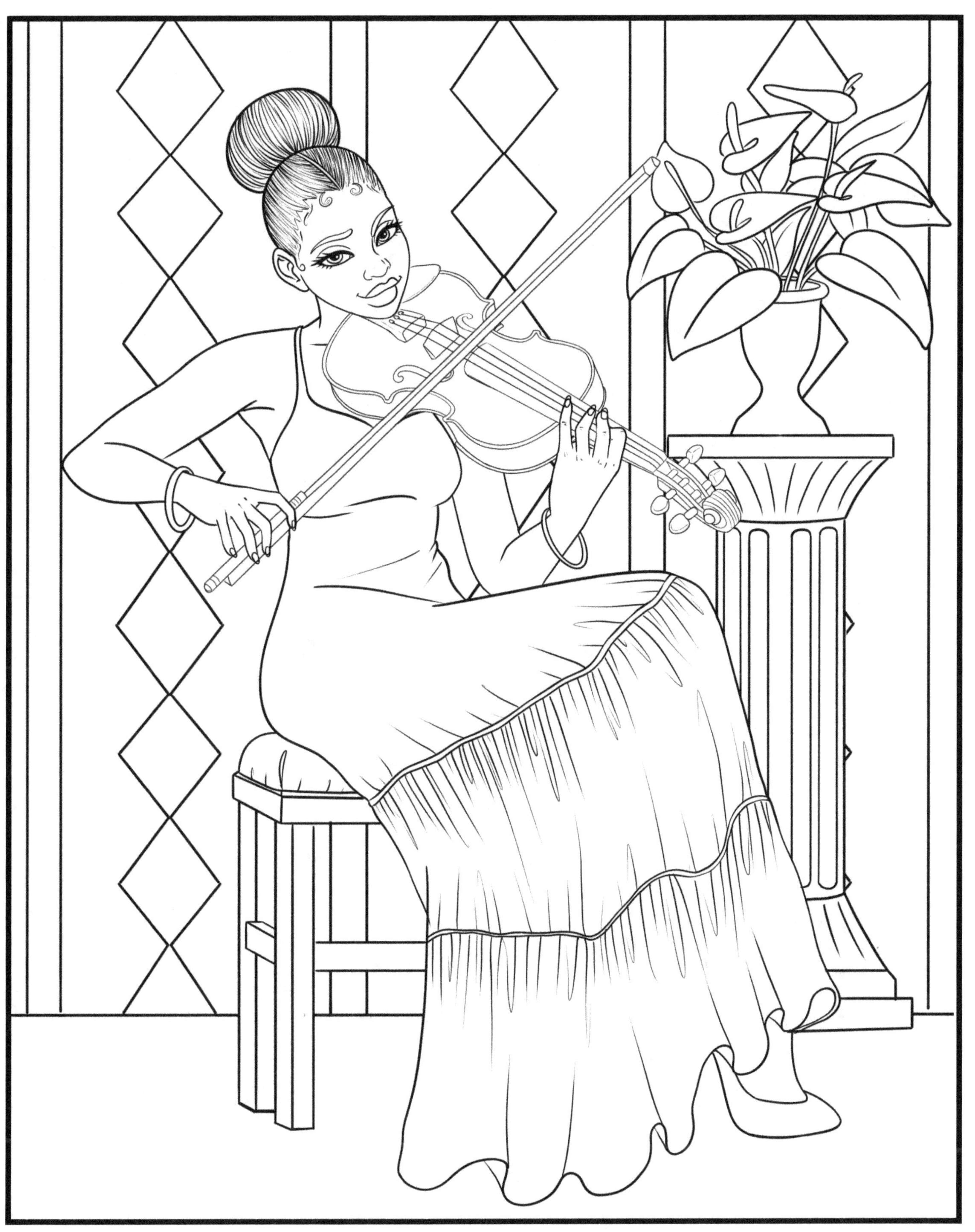

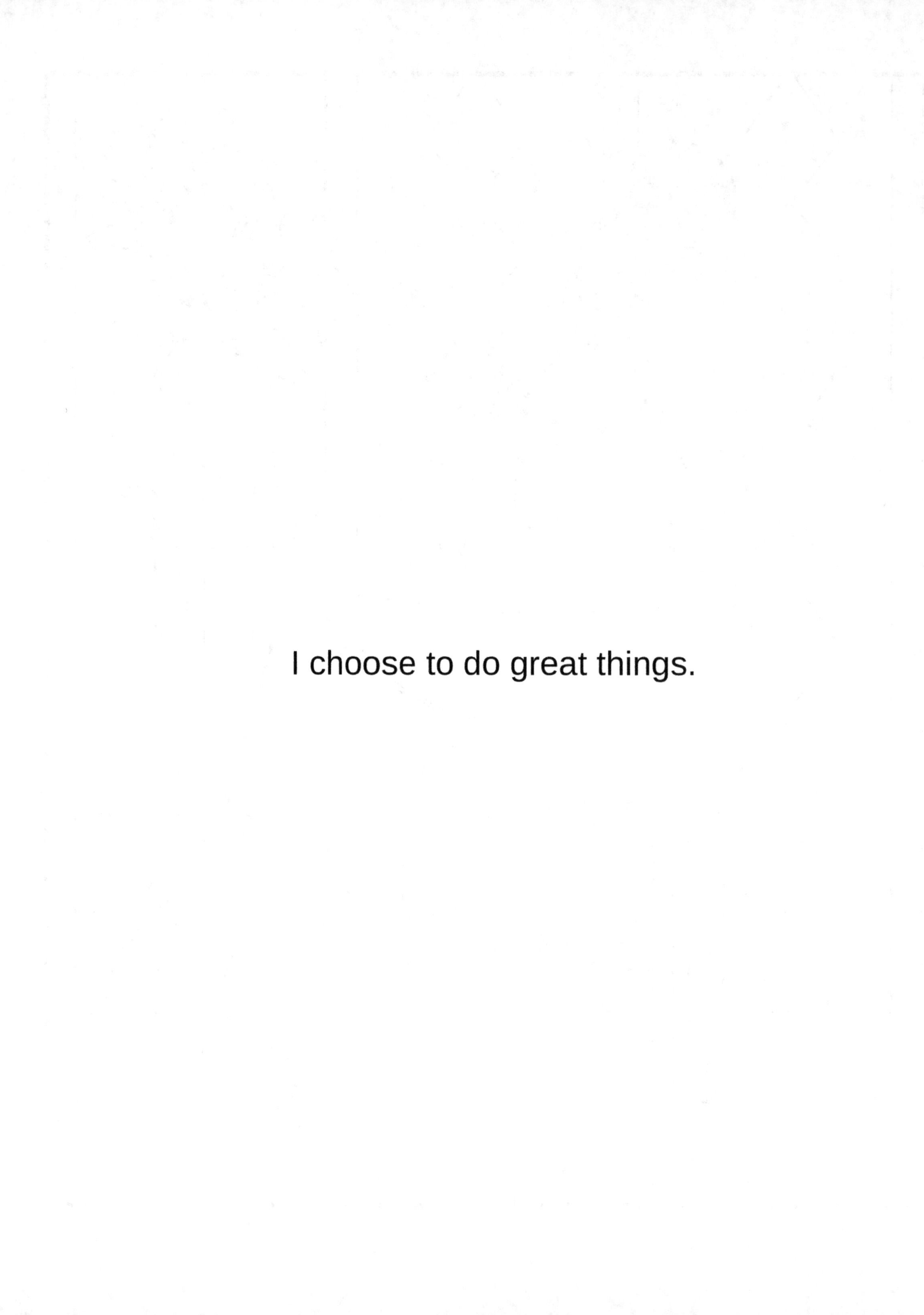

I choose to do great things.

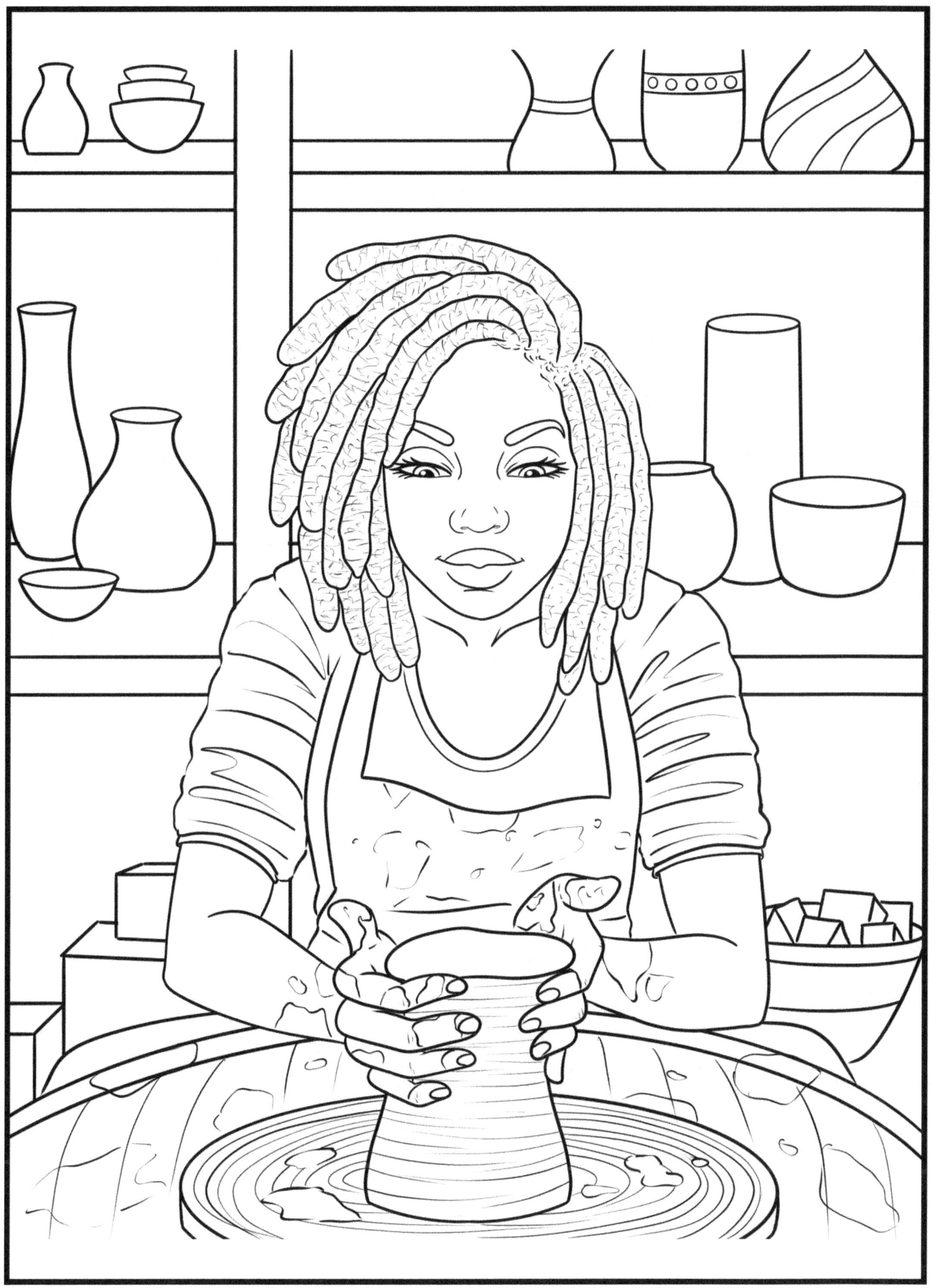

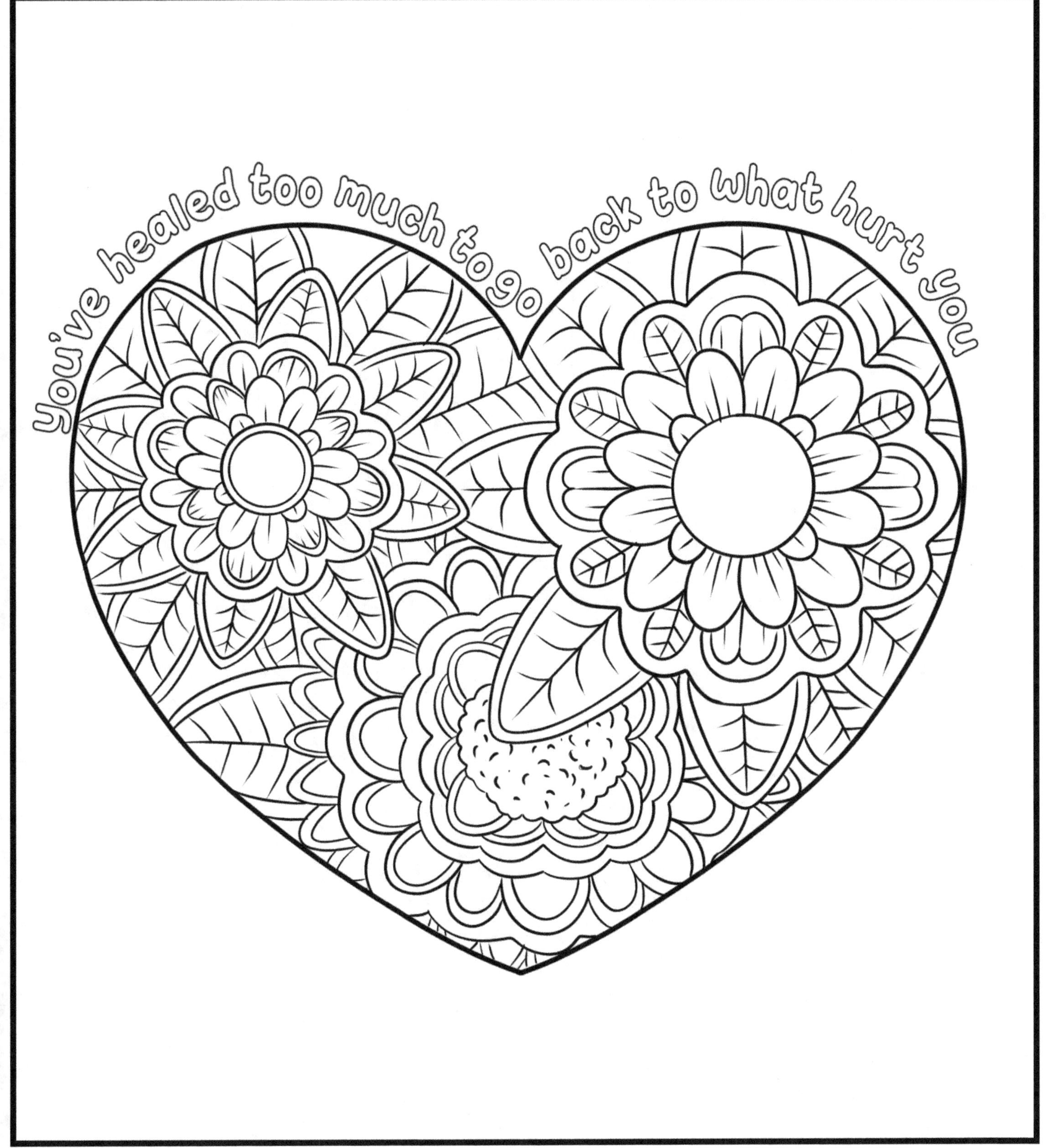
you've healed too much to go back to what hurt you

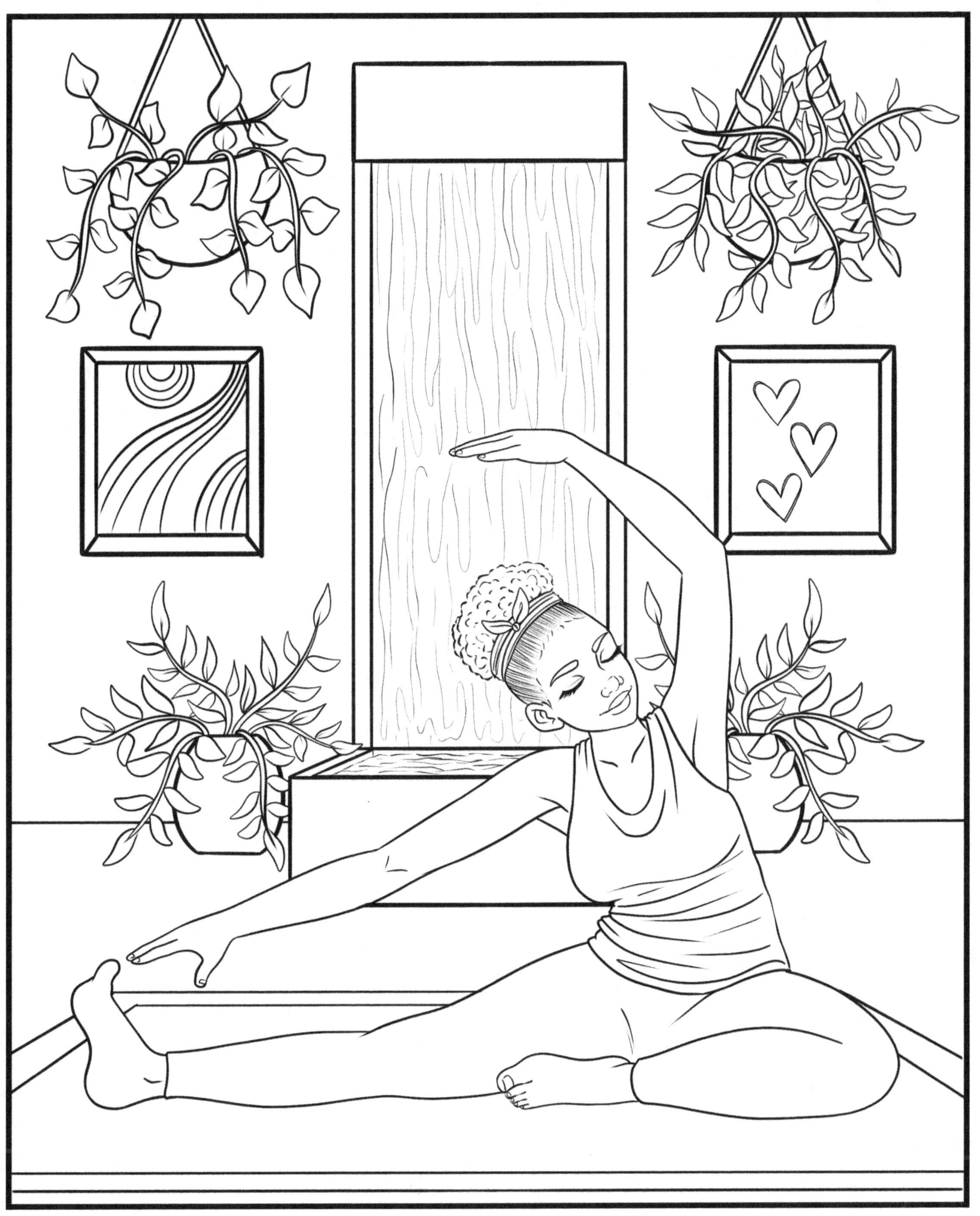

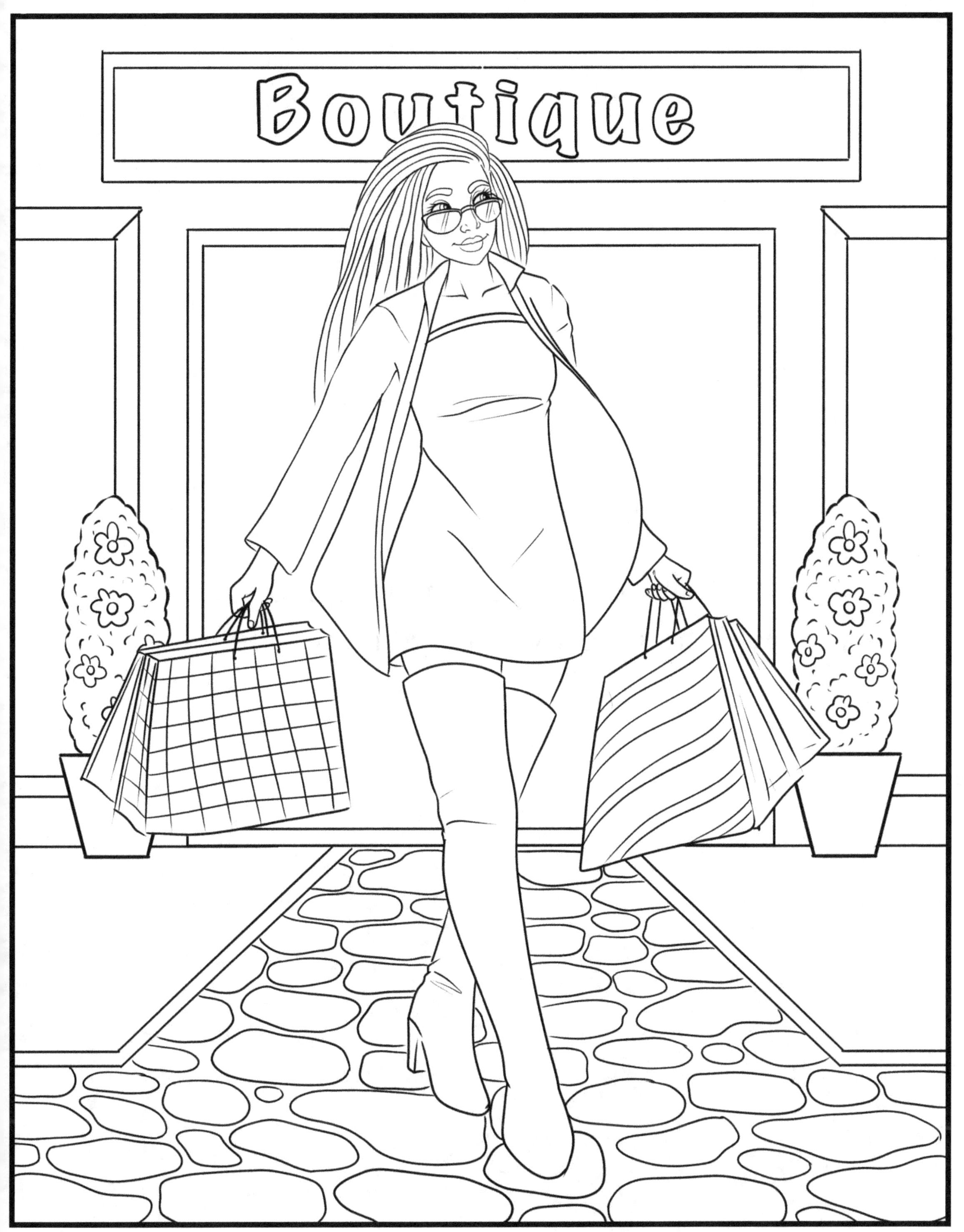
Boutique

Think on things that are good.
Refuse to believe everything you feel.

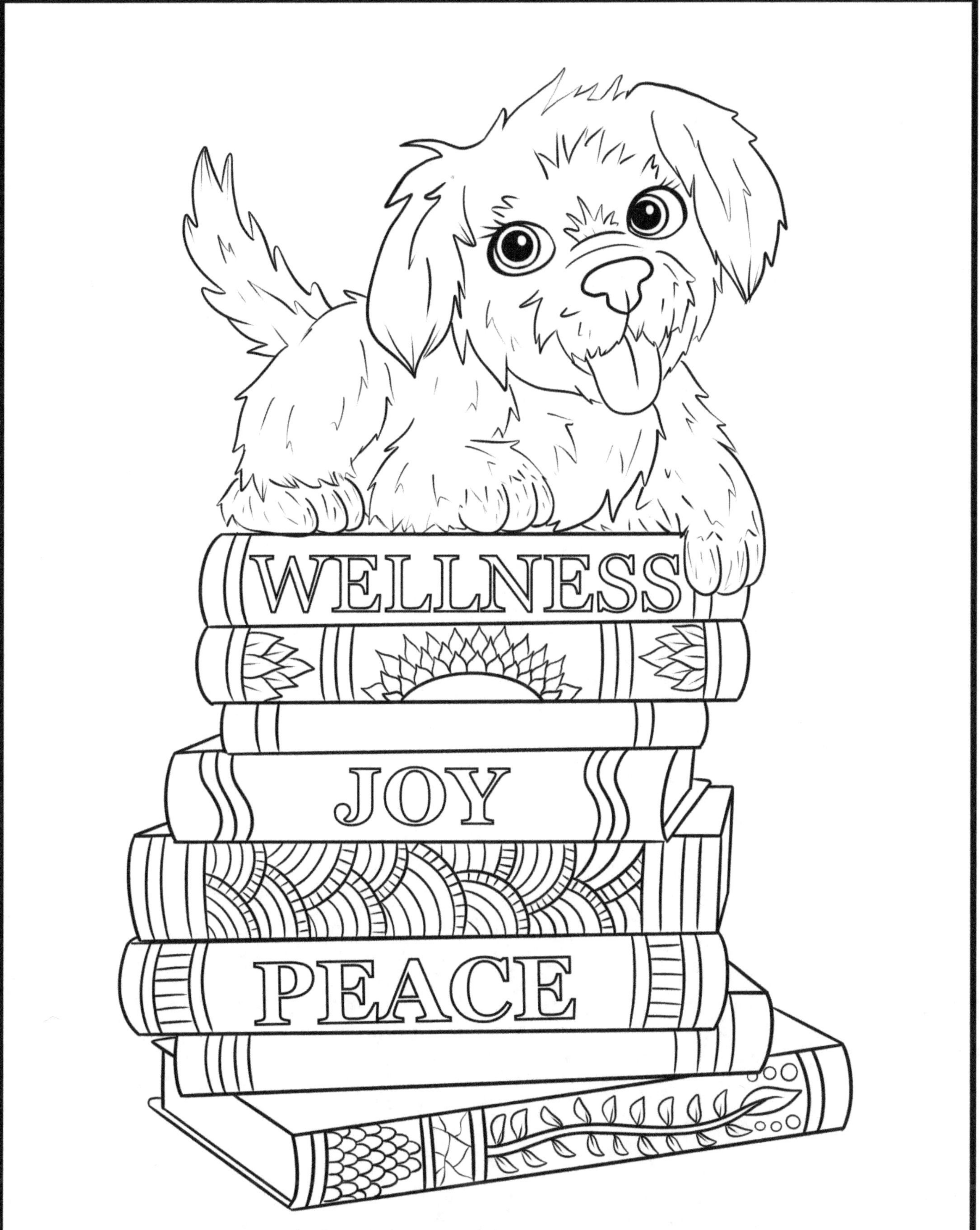

WELLNESS
JOY
PEACE

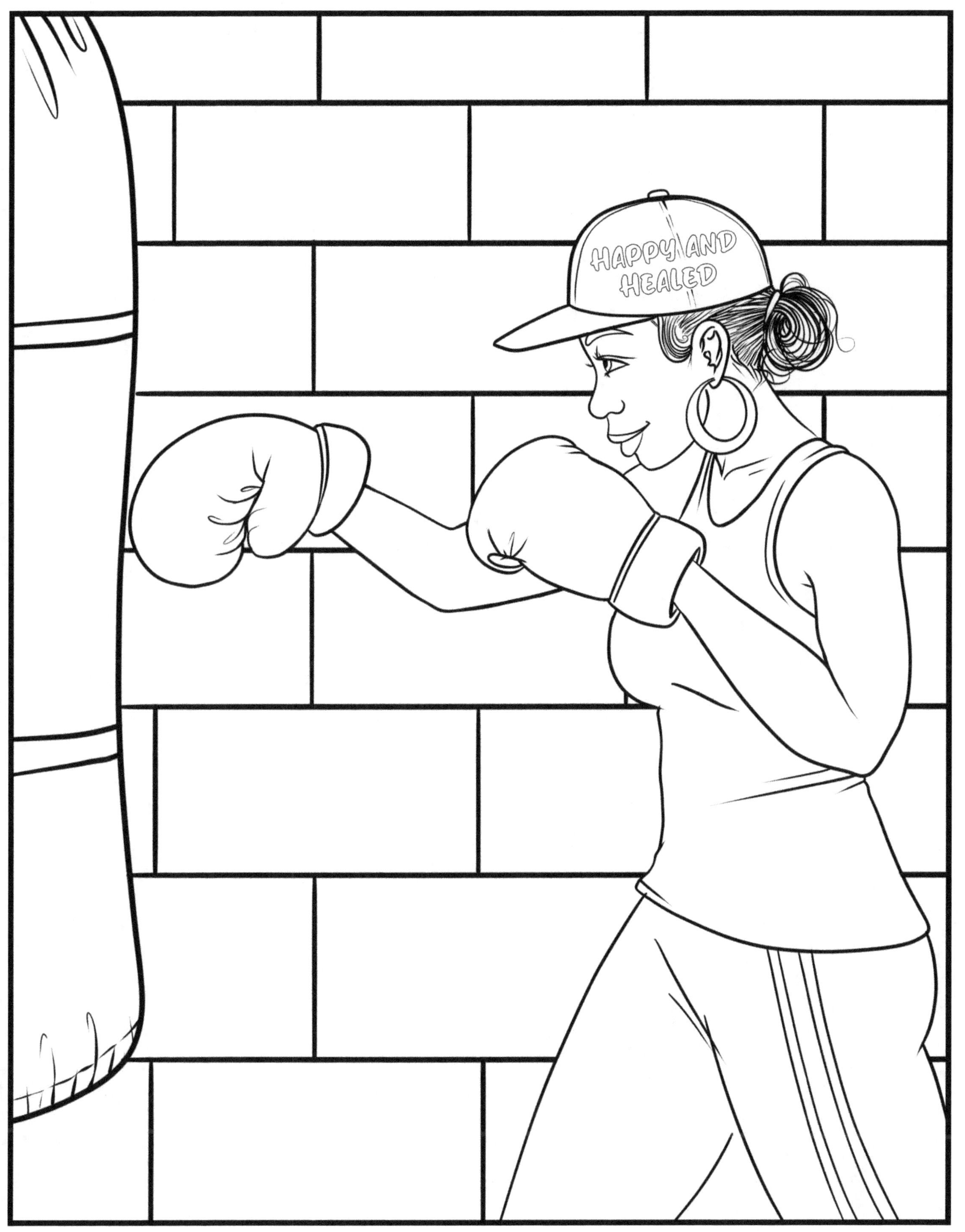

HAPPY AND HEALED

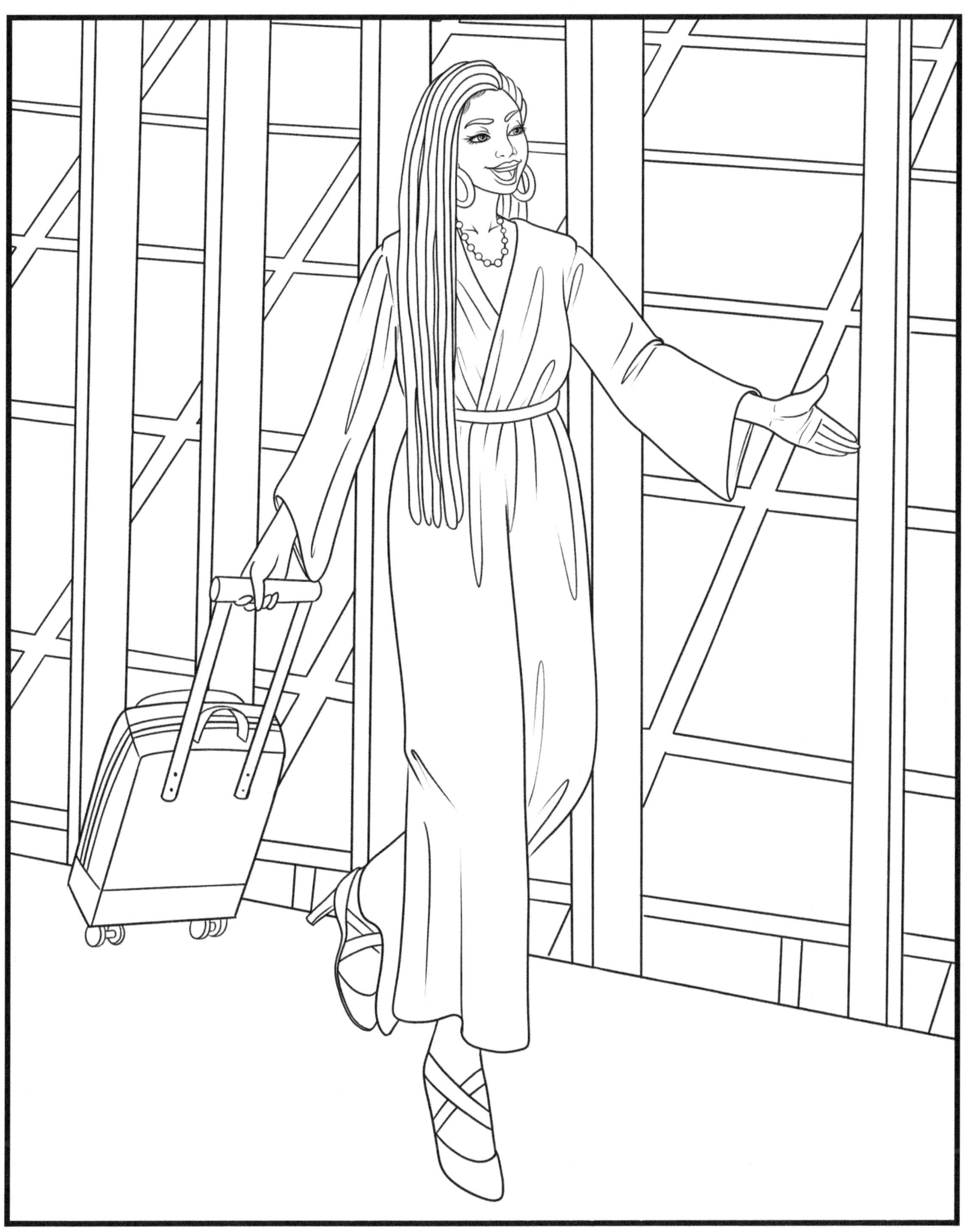

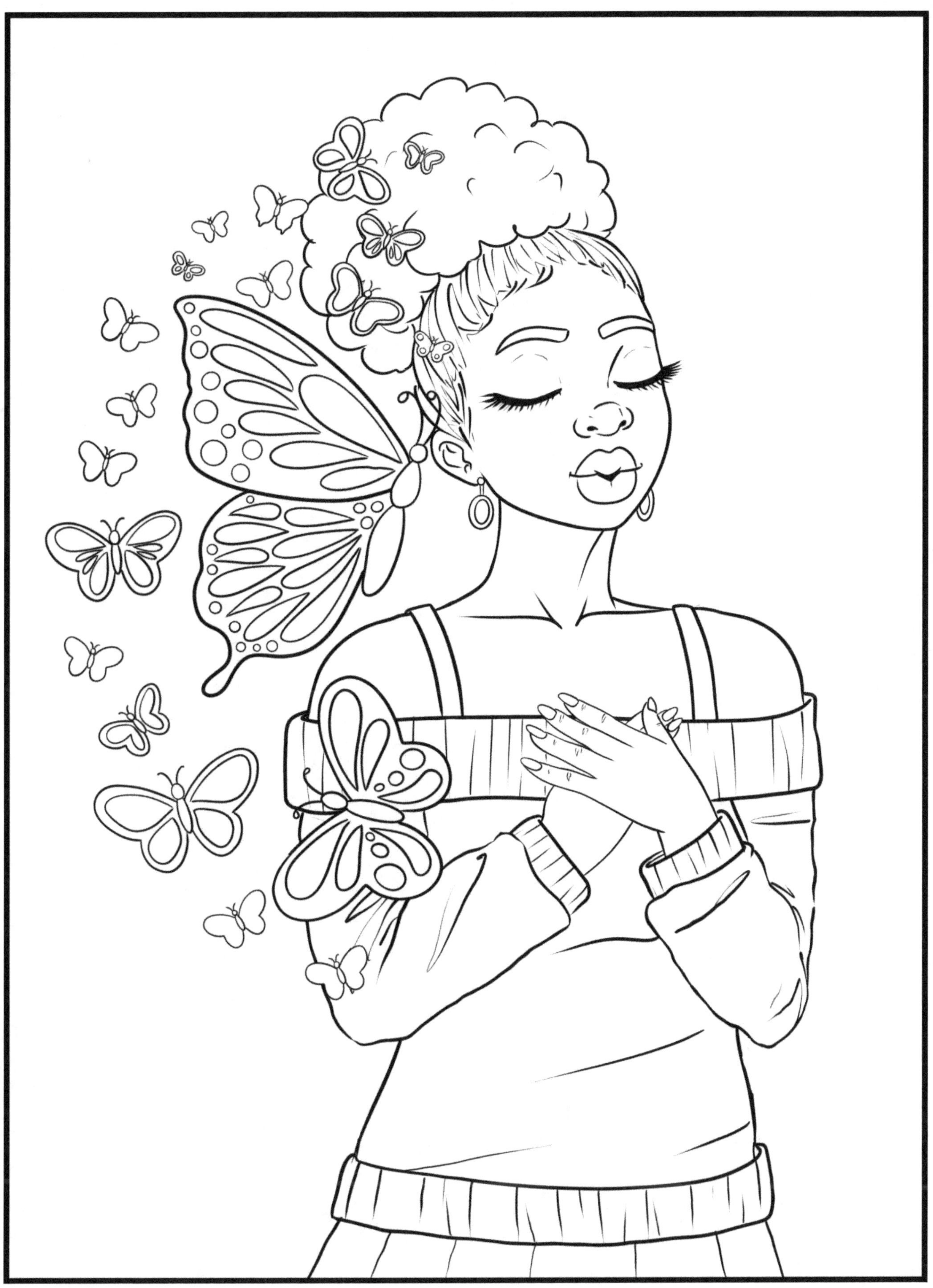